SHALLOW CHRISTIANITY?
A STUDY IN HEBREWS
Chapters 1-3

Mark Driscoll

Shallow Christianity? A Study in Hebrews. Chapters 1-3
© 2024 by Mark Driscoll

ISBN: 978-1-966223-03-0 (Paperback)
ISBN: 978-1-966223-04-7 (E-book)

Scripture quotations are from the ESV® Bible (The Holy Bible, English Standard Version®), copyright © 2001 by Crossway, a publishing ministry of Good News Publishers. Used by permission. All rights reserved. The ESV text may not be quoted in any publication made available to the public by a Creative Commons license. The ESV may not be translated in whole or in part into any other language.

All emphases in Scripture quotations have been added by the author.

No part of this publication may be reproduced, stored in a retrieval system, or transmitted in any form by any means, electronic, mechanical, photocopy, recording, or otherwise, without the prior permission of the publisher, except as provided for by USA copyright law.

CONTENTS

Real Groups	1
Chapter 1: Digging into Hebrews	3
Chapter 2: Hitting Bedrock in the Old Testament	9
Chapter 3: 10 Tips for Studying Hebrews	21
Chapter 4: Hebrews 1-3 Personal and Group Study Guide	29
1 – Hebrews 1:1-14	29
How Can I Hear From God?	
2 – Hebrews 2:1-9	35
Why is God Angry with Shallow Christians?	
3 – Hebrews 2:10-18	40
How Do I Overcome Suffering and Temptation?	
4 – Hebrews 3:1-6	47
How is Jesus the Hero of the Whole Bible?	
5 – Hebrews 3:7-19	53
Does God Punish Some Believers?	
About Pastor Mark & RealFaith	59
More Resources	61

REAL GROUPS
WITH REALFAITH

Faith that does not result in good deeds is not real faith.
— James 2:20 (TLB)

At RealFaith, we believe that the Word of God isn't just for us to read, it's to be obeyed. And living in community with fellow believers is one of the ways God the Father allows us to learn and grow to become more like His Son Jesus through the power of the Holy Spirit. We do this through something called Real Groups. Here are a few tips to start your own.

1. Invite
Invite your friends, neighbors, family, coworkers, and enemies, because they all need Jesus whether they know Him or not! Whether it's a group of men, women, families, students, or singles, explain that you'd like to start a weekly sermon-based small group based on Pastor Mark Driscoll's sermons.

2. Listen to the sermon on realfaith.com or on the RealFaith app
You can host a viewing party to watch RealFaith Live and discuss it all at once, or you can watch it separately and gather to discuss it at another time that works for the group.

3. Get into God's Word
In addition to watching the sermon, make sure you and all group members have a study guide from realfaith.com for the current sermon series. There are questions for personal reflection as well as for groups that can guide your devotional times throughout the week. You can also sign up for Daily Devos at **realfaith.com**.

4. Gather together

Whether at someone's house, a public place, or through something like Zoom, meet weekly to discuss the sermon and what God has taught you through it. The great thing about Real Groups is that you don't all have to be in the same location. You can talk about sermon takeaways, what stood out to you in the study guide, or what God taught you in His Word that week. Focus on personal application as much as possible.

5. Pray

When you gather, feel free to share prayer requests, pray for each other on the spot, and continue praying throughout the week. Prayer is a great unifying force that God gives us to strengthen His family.

6. Share

Send us photos, videos, testimonies, and updates of how your group is doing to **hello@realfaith.com**. You might even be featured on our RealFaith Live show!

We will be praying for you and your group and look forward to hearing what God does through it.

CHAPTER 1
DIGGING INTO HEBREWS

Where I live in the Arizona desert, the monsoon season brings strong winds and heavy rains. Once the storms subside, the damage is visible everywhere. Because the soil is clay and water is sparse, the roots for trees and cactuses are very shallow. In fact, it is not uncommon for a tall cactus to be held up by only a few inches of roots. Everything is fine until a storm comes. When a storm hits, trees and cactuses are uprooted in great numbers, lying on their sides rather than remaining upright. Sadly, too many Christians are the same. Due to little Bible teaching and less obedience, their roots are so shallow that when a stormy season of trouble and turmoil hits, they are blown over because their faith is shallow.

The good news for Christians is that God wants to help us deepen our roots. If we do, then we can withstand the storms of life, not getting blown over when life sends us a big storm. There is one book in the Bible that is specifically written to help you dig deeper into God's Word, sinking the roots of your faith into the unshakable soil of Jesus Christ.

For starters, the book of Hebrews is written to believers who have endured a pounding stormy season and did not fare well because their roots were shallow. Does this sound familiar? Your church attendance, prayer life, and Bible reading seem to hold you up...until the storm comes. Your marriage hits a crisis, your kids are struggling, you lose your job, your health takes a turn, or some other crisis hits your life, knocking you over and ripping the roots of your faith right out of the ground. Have you ever wondered if God is real, if your faith is worth the effort, or if you can keep trusting God much longer? If so, then you know how hard life becomes during a storm and what it feels like to have a shallow-rooted faith.

Hebrews speaks to believers over and over, instructing us to not get uprooted when the storms of life hit:
- 2:1 – Therefore we must pay much closer attention to what we have heard, lest we drift away from it.

- 3:6 – And we are his house, if indeed we hold fast our confidence and our boasting in our hope.
- 3:14 – …we have come to share in Christ, if indeed we hold our original confidence firm to the end.
- 6:9-12 – Though we speak in this way, yet in your case, beloved, we feel sure of better things—things that belong to salvation. For God is not unjust so as to overlook your work and the love that you have shown for his name in serving the saints, as you still do. And we desire each one of you to show the same earnestness to have the full assurance of hope until the end, so that you may not be sluggish, but imitators of those who through faith and patience inherit the promises.
- 10:23 – Let us hold fast the confession of our hope without wavering, for he who promised is faithful.
- 10:32-36 – But recall the former days when, after you were enlightened, you endured a hard struggle with sufferings, sometimes being publicly exposed to reproach and affliction, and sometimes being partners with those so treated. For you had compassion on those in prison, and you joyfully accepted the plundering of your property, since you knew that you yourselves had a better possession and an abiding one. Therefore do not throw away your confidence, which has a great reward. For you have need of endurance, so that when you have done the will of God you may receive what is promised.
- 10:39 – But we are not of those who shrink back and are destroyed, but of those who have faith and preserve their souls.

One of the main purposes of the book, according to Hebrews 13:22, is exhortation: "I appeal to you, brothers, bear with my word of exhortation, for I have written to you briefly." If you've even seen a coach firing up a team for a big game, watched a politician rally a crowd for action, or seen a commanding officer put steel in the spine of soldiers before sending them off on a mission, then you get the gist of what is meant by exhortation. As believers, we can and do get a bit lazy and lethargic, distracted and discouraged, and Hebrews is the Holy Spirit's way of getting our full attention, refocusing our priorities, and creating a sense of urgency for God and the things of God!

Over and over, the book of Hebrews teaches us that our Christian faith can improve because God in Jesus Christ makes everything "better."[a] Our relationship with God, like any relationship, can always get better. There is always something new to learn, improvements to make, and trust to build. God wants your study of Hebrews to help your faith in Him and your relationship with Him to get better and better. If your faith is weak, it can and will get stronger. If your faith is strong, it can get even stronger. No matter how mature or immature your faith is, there is always room for your roots to go deeper. The book of Hebrews repeatedly reminds us that we cannot settle but must constantly strive to increase our understanding of and trust in God. Although we will never achieve it in this life, our goal is to walk one step every day towards the eternal version of our faith, which is "perfect."[b]

A Bible commentary says,

> The main message of Hebrews is summarized in 6:1: "let us go on unto perfection [spiritual maturity]." The people to whom Hebrews was addressed were not growing spiritually (5:11–14) and were in a state of second childhood. God had spoken in the Word, but they were not faithful to obey Him. They were neglecting God's instruction and drifting away from His blessing. The writer seeks to encourage them to move ahead in their spiritual lives by showing them that in Christ they have the "better" blessings. He is the "author and perfecter [finisher] of our faith" (12:2). The book presents the Christian faith and life as superior to Judaism or any other religious system. Christ is the superior Person (1–6); His Priesthood is superior to that of Aaron (7–10); and the principle of faith is superior to that of law (11–13).[1]

Are you tired of a shallow faith that hasn't grown in recent years like it should have? Do you miss the zeal you had for God in a past season that has grown a bit cold? Has

---

[a] 1:4; 6:9; 7:7, 19, 22; 8:6; 9:23; 10:34; 11:16, 35, 40; 12:24 [b] 2:10; 5:9; 7:11, 19, 28; 9:9, 11; 10:1, 14; 11:40; 12:2, 23

life brought you more questions and new struggles that you need new understanding to overcome and endure? Does your Christian faith feel like it's on autopilot, and are you often just going through the motions? Do you get the sense that a lot of the Bible teaching you've had is like a weak barbecue sauce that has been so watered down that it's lost its flavor? If this sounds like you, then Hebrews has some passionate, enthusiastic, and urgent invitations. When you read the Bible humbly and expectantly, the most amazing thing happens. The author meets with you to help you learn and apply what was written. This is precisely what Hebrews 4:12 means, saying, "For the word of God is living and active, sharper than any two-edged sword, piercing to the division of soul and of spirit, of joints and of marrow, and discerning the thoughts and intentions of the heart." Because God the Holy Spirit wrote the Scriptures through human authors, He will meet with you as you study Hebrews to understand what it says (information) and give you power in the Spirit to obey what it says (impartation), which changes your life and legacy (transformation).

If you are ready to stop settling for a shallow faith and dig your roots deep in Hebrews, the following invitations should motivate you to urgently and passionately take God the Spirit up on His repeated invitations throughout Hebrews:

- 4:14-16 – Since then we have a great high priest who has passed through the heavens, Jesus, the Son of God, let us hold fast our confession. For we do not have a high priest who is unable to sympathize with our weaknesses, but one who in every respect has been tempted as we are, yet without sin. Let us then with confidence draw near to the throne of grace, that we may receive mercy and find grace to help in time of need.
- 6:1 – Therefore let us leave the elementary doctrine of Christ and go on to maturity, not laying again a foundation of repentance from dead works and of faith toward God…
- 10:22-24 – …let us draw near with a true heart in full assurance of faith, with our hearts sprinkled clean from

an evil conscience and our bodies washed with pure water. Let us hold fast the confession of our hope without wavering, for he who promised is faithful. And let us consider how to stir up one another to love and good works...
- 12:1-3 – Therefore, since we are surrounded by so great a cloud of witnesses, let us also lay aside every weight, and sin which clings so closely, and let us run with endurance the race that is set before us, looking to Jesus, the founder and perfecter of our faith, who for the joy that was set before him endured the cross, despising the shame, and is seated at the right hand of the throne of God. Consider him who endured from sinners such hostility against himself, so that you may not grow weary or fainthearted.

If you want to dig your roots deeper, you must go all the way back to the Old Testament. Sadly, most Christians know far too little about the Old Testament.

When Christians make enormous claims about the Bible, they are in fact simply restating what the Bible says about itself. The Bible asserts that God authored the entire book down to every word. It also claims God did this through human authors. These authors retained their own style, voice, perspective, and cultural distinctives, yet God uniquely inspired them to write down what He wanted recorded with complete accuracy. This makes the Bible unique from, superior to, and in authority over everyone and everything else on the earth, because when the Bible speaks, God speaks.

Scripture is God speaking His truth to us in human words. The New Testament writers claim that the Old Testament is sacred Scripture, which literally means "writing."[a] The word Bible comes from the Greek word for book. Holy Bible means "Holy Book." It was written in three languages (Hebrew, Greek, and a bit in Aramaic) over a period of more than 1500 years by roughly 40 authors (of varying ages and backgrounds) on three continents (Asia,

---

[a] Matt. 21:42, 22:29, 26:54,56; Luke 24:25-32, 44-45; John 5:39, 10:35; Acts 17:2,11; 18:28; Rom. 1:2, 4:3, 9:17, 10:11, 11:2, 15:4, 16:26; 1 Cor. 15:3-4; Gal. 3:8,22, 4:30; 1 Tim. 5:18; 2 Tim. 3:16; James 4:5; 2 Pet. 1:20-21, 3:15-16

Africa, and Europe).

The Protestant Canon of the Bible contains 66 separate books. 39 books, approximately three-quarters of the Bible, are in the Old Testament, which is a record of God's speaking and working in history from when he created Adam and Eve up until about 450 BC. In the period between the two testaments, people waited for the coming of the Messiah into human history. The 27 books of the New Testament begin with the four Gospels, which record the life, death, burial, Resurrection, and ascension (return to Heaven) of Jesus and then proceed to instruct Christians and churches about how to think and live for God.

Roughly three-quarters of the Christian Bible is the Old Testament. The Old Testament has 929 chapters and 23,214 verses. The New Testament has 260 chapters and 7,959 verses. In the Old Testament, the longest book is Psalms, and the shortest book is Obadiah. In the New Testament, the longest book is Acts, and the shortest book is 3 John.

The Bible is a library of books compiled as one Book, showing a divine unity and continuity. This point is illustrated by the fact that the New Testament has roughly 300 explicit Old Testament quotations, as well as upwards of 4,000 allusions to the Old Testament. In many ways, the Old Testament is a series of promises that God makes, and the New Testament is the record of their fulfillment and anticipation of the final fulfillment of the remaining promises at Jesus' Second Coming.

As you read the Old Testament, you must remember that your position in history is not entirely unlike the Old Testament believers. They read the Old Testament in faith, anticipating the first coming of Jesus to fulfill the promises of the Old Testament. We now read both the Old and New Testaments in faith, eagerly awaiting the Second Coming of Jesus to fulfill the remaining promises of Scripture given to His people.

The Old Testament is the Bible that Jesus learned as a boy, memorized, quoted, and taught from. There is simply no way to root your faith deeper without digging into the Old Testament. The book of Hebrews is uniquely written to help you do this very thing, as we will learn next.

CHAPTER 2
HITTING BEDROCK IN THE OLD TESTAMENT

On a recent visit to a doctor's office, when one of the male nurses found out I was a pastor, he started sharing his testimony of becoming a Christian in recent years and how Jesus changed his life. He also said he was enjoying reading the Bible but felt a bit lost when reading the Old Testament. He said he appreciated the history of the Jewish people and God using them to bring us the prophets, Scriptures, and Jesus Christ. He wanted to better understand the Hebrew roots of our faith but struggled to make sense of Old Testament themes like animal sacrifices, holiness codes, and the priesthood. I appreciated his honesty, and the truth is most Christians likely feel the exact same way and struggle with the exact same questions.

How about you? Have you ever started reading the Old Testament and felt like you were a bit lost, like a tourist to a foreign culture that was a mystery to you? If you've ever traveled to another country or spent some time with a friend group in your own hometown from a different culture, you know it's very helpful to have someone come alongside you as a translator and tour guide to explain, in terms you can understand, the new world you have entered into.

In the New Testament, there is an ongoing series of debates between two groups of people —the Jews and the Gentiles —present in most every book. The Old Testament is written by, and primarily about and for, the Hebrew Jews. Jesus and His disciples were also Jews. Over time there was a greater shift in early Christian identity from Jewish Christianity to Gentile Christianity. A Bible commentary says,

> Although Jewish attitudes toward Gentiles were diverse, Jews always placed limits on interactions with Gentiles (e.g., no intermarriage, no idolatry, no entry by Gentiles into central courts of the temple). These sorts of

ew out of Israel's holiness laws and
 ide evangelizing Gentiles unnatural for
 ely, the intensity of the early church's
 on grew from several factors...(1) a
 o declare religious views in public; (2) the
impact of Jesus' words in the Great Commission (Matt 28:16–20) and at His ascension (Acts 1:8); (3) the dispute over what to do with early Gentile converts (see Acts 15:1–35); (4) Gentiles attending Jewish synagogues who were receptive to hearing about Jesus; (5) the dispersion of Jews from the land of Israel to surrounding Gentile lands; (6) reflection by Jewish Christians on the Scriptures and the place of Gentiles; (7) the powerful experience of the Holy Spirit in the early church that prompted further outreach.[2]

Today, most Christians around the world are not Jewish but rather Gentiles. We do not trace our family history to Abraham and Sarah and are not familiar with all the customs and traditions that find many of their origins in the Old Testament for the simple reason our history and ancestry is from elsewhere. A Bible Dictionary says, "'Gentiles' is the common English translation of the Greek term *ethnē*, which in Paul and elsewhere in the NT [New Testament] is used to refer to nations other than the nation of Israel."[3]

Most Gentile Christians have a great appreciation for the Jewish people but struggle to understand how the Old Covenant found in the Old Testament applies to Gentiles in the New Covenant found in the New Testament. There is one book in the Bible that is most helpful for resolving this problem, serving as a bridge of sorts between the Old and New Covenants and Testaments, connecting everyone and everything to Jesus Christ —Hebrews.

When I was a kid, I made the mistake of removing the spokes of my bike wheel from the hub to see what would happen. Not surprisingly, that simple series of moves wrecked my wheel and made it impossible to ride my bike. When studying the Old Testament, everyone and everything are like the spokes, and Jesus Christ must be the hub; otherwise, there's no way to hold it all together. Just as Jesus is the hero and subject of the New Testament, the same is true in the Old Testament. Over and over, the book of Hebrews continually refers to people, events, roles, themes, and stories from the Old Testament. In addition, Hebrews directly quotes the Old Testament repeatedly, quoting those verses from the Septuagint, which is the Old Testament translated into Greek[4]:

Number	Hebrews	Old Testament Scripture(s) (LXX = Septuagint)
1	1:5a	Psalm 2:7
2	1:5b	2 Samuel 7:14 (= 1 Chronicles 17:13)
3	1:6	Deuteronomy 32:43 LXX and Psalm 96:7 LXX (English 97:7)
4	1:7	Psalm 103:4 LXX (English 104:4)
5	1:8–9	Psalm 44:7–8 LXX (English 45:6–7)
6	1:10–12	Psalm 101:26–28 LXX (English 102:25b–27)
7	1:13	Psalm 109:1 LXX (English 110:1)
8	2:8	Psalm 8:5–7 LXX (English 8:4–6)
9	2:12	Psalm 21:23 LXX (English 22:22)
10	2:13a	Isaiah 8:17 (compare Isa 12:2; 2 Sam 22:3b LXX)
11	2:13b	Isaiah 8:18
12	3:7–11	Psalm 95:7b–11
13	3:15	Psalm 95:7b–8a
14	4:3b	Psalm 95:11

Number	Hebrews	Old Testament Scripture(s) (LXX = Septuagint)
15	4:4b	Genesis 2:2
16	4:5	Psalm 95:11b
17	4:7b	Psalm 95:7b
18	5:5	Psalm 2:7
19	5:6	Psalm 110:4
20	6:14	Genesis 22:17
21	7:1–2	Genesis 14:17–19
22	7:4	Genesis 14:20
23	7:17	Psalm 110:4
24	7:21	Psalm 110:4
25	8:5b	Exodus 25:40
26	8:8–12	Jeremiah 31:31–34
27	9:20	Exodus 24:8
28	10:5–7	Psalm 39:7–9 LXX (English 40:6–8)
29	10:8	Psalm 39:7 LXX (English 40:6)
30	10:9	Psalm 39:9 LXX (English 40:8)
31	10:16–17	Jeremiah 31:33–34
32	10:28	Deuteronomy 17:6
33	10:30a	Deuteronomy 32:35
34	10:30b	Deuteronomy 32:36 LXX (compare Psalm 134:14 LXX [English 135:14])
35	10:37a	Isaiah 26:20 LXX (μικρὸν ὅσον ὅσον, *mikron hoson* hoson)

Number	Hebrews	Old Testament Scripture(s) (LXX = Septuagint)
36	10:37b	Habakkuk 2:3b
37	10:38a, b	Habakkuk 2:4b, a
38	11:18	Genesis 21:17b
39	11:21b	Genesis 47:31b LXX: "staff" (Hebrew: "bed")
40	12:5–6	Proverbs 3:11–12
41	12:15b	Deuteronomy 29:17b LXX (English 29:18b)
42	12:15	Deuteronomy 9:19
43	12:21	Deuteronomy 9:19
44	12:26b	Haggai 2:6, 21
45	12:29	Deuteronomy 4:24; 9:3
46	13:5	Deuteronomy 6, 8; Gen 28:15
47	13:6	Psalm 117:6 LXX (English: 118:6)

The most quoted Old Testament Scripture in Hebrews is Psalm 110, which begins by promising the current sovereign rule and reign of Jesus Christ over everyone and everything, saying, "The LORD says to my Lord: 'Sit at my right hand, until I make your enemies your footstool.'" Perhaps the central Old Testament Scripture in Hebrews that connects every theme and thread to Jesus Christ and the New Covenant is Jeremiah 31:31-34,

> Behold, the days are coming, declares the LORD, when I will make a new covenant with the house of Israel and the house of Judah, not like the covenant that I made with their fathers on the day when I took them by the hand to bring them out of the land of Egypt, my c ovenant that they broke, though I was their husband, declares the LORD. For this is the covenant that I will

make with the house of Israel after those days, declares the LORD: I will put my law within them, and I will write it on their hearts. And I will be their God, and they shall be my people. And no longer shall each one teach his neighbor and each his brother, saying, "Know the LORD," for they shall all know me, from the least of them to the greatest, declares the LORD. For I will forgive their iniquity, and I will remember their sin no more.

Unlike previous covenants (Noahic, Abrahamic, Mosaic, Davidic), the New Covenant is God not merely giving us a human mediator but the second member of the Trinity Himself coming into human history as the man Jesus Christ. Rather than taking life as He did when He flooded the earth in the days of Noah or requiring sacrifices for sin in the Mosaic covenant, He offered Himself as the sacrificial substitute for sinners on the cross, where He shed His blood in their place.

In the New Covenant, God comes to be with each of His people as He did with Noah, Abraham, Moses, and David. He also places the Holy Spirit in them to make them into a temple where worship occurs. The Spirit makes them new creations as the dawning and firstfruits of the finality of the new creation that culminates with Jesus' second coming. The Spirit's work includes transfiguring us into Jesus' image bearers, as Moses was.

Perhaps the lengthiest treatment of the New Covenant and its superiority to all preceding covenants is found in the book of Hebrews. In light of our study of covenants, the most helpful thing would be to simply read Hebrews 8:6-9:28.

Too many Christians wrongly think that the Old Testament is just that —old, outdated, archaic, no longer relevant, and does not apply to them. Some of the devaluation of the Old Testament may be caused by its very title. It was the early church father Origen (185–254) who first coined the phrases Old and New Testaments. Prior to this designation, the Jews and early Church would have only known what we call the Old Testament as the Law, the Prophets, and the Writings, or the Scriptures. Origen's confusion came from misunderstanding Jeremiah's use of the Old and New Covenants in Jeremiah 31:31. By "new," Jeremiah did not mean something detached from the prior works of God but something renewed or fulfilled. Therefore, the New Covenant is the renewal or fulfillment of the old. The Old and New Testaments are equally inspired by God and important to the Christian life. 2 Timothy 3:16-17 says, "All Scripture is breathed out by God and profitable for teaching, for reproof, for correction, and for training in righteousness, that the man of God may be complete, equipped for every good work." Since many of the books of the New Testament had not been written, this Scripture obviously refers in large part to all of the Old Testament.

Likewise, the New Testament is inextricably linked to the Old Testament as its renewed fulfillment. By way of example, God's people in the Old Testament received saving grace from God in the same way that Christians in the New Testament do, simply by having faith in God's promises that Jesus would pay the penalty for sin through the cross and empty tomb.[a] In an amazing illustration of just how the New Testament is the renewed fulfillment of the promises of the Old Testament, Paul says that Abraham believed by faith that his seed (Jesus) would save him—and this is the gospel (or good news) about Jesus Christ that Christians today still trust.[b]

Both the Old and New Testaments are about the same God. The opening line of Scripture introduces us to its Hero, God, who is revealed throughout the rest of the pages of Scripture. In the closing line of the New Testament, we are reminded that our hope is in "...the grace of the Lord Jesus..."[c] Thus, the written Word of God reveals to us the incarnate ("in human flesh") Word of God, Jesus Christ. Without the written Word, we cannot rightly know the incarnate Word.

The Old and New Testaments are about Jesus Christ — anyone can read the Bible, but only someone who reads it in the Spirit comes to this rightful conclusion. Some prefer the New Testament to the Old Testament because they wrongly believe that only the New Testament is about Jesus. However, Jesus Himself taught that the Old Testament was primarily about Him while arguing with the theologians

[a] Hebrews 11 [b] Galatians 3:8,14 [c] Revelation 22:21

in his day. In John 5:39-40, Jesus says, "You search the Scriptures [Old Testament] because you think that in them you have eternal life; and it is they that bear witness about me, yet you refuse to come to me that you may have life." The Bible is not just principles to live by but a Person to live with.

Following His Resurrection, Jesus opened the Old Testament to teach about Himself: "...beginning with Moses and all the Prophets, he interpreted to them in all the Scriptures the things concerning himself."[a] Likewise, in speaking to His disciples, Jesus said, "These are my words that I spoke to you while I was still with you, that everything written about me in the Law of Moses and the Prophets and the Psalms must be fulfilled."[b] We then read that He "...opened their minds to understand the Scriptures..."[c] Jesus' own words about Himself as the central message of the Old Testament are pointedly clear. He said in Matthew 5:17-18,

> Do not think that I have come to abolish the Law or the Prophets; I have not come to abolish them but to fulfill them. For truly, I say to you, until heaven and earth pass away, not an iota, not a dot, will pass from the Law until all is accomplished.

Jesus repeated this fact throughout His ministry by saying He "fulfilled" particular Scriptures.[d] To correctly interpret Scripture, you will need to connect its verses, concepts, and events to Jesus.

The Old Testament predicts the coming of Jesus in a variety of ways to prepare people. The New Testament reflects back on the life of Jesus, particularly in the four Gospels, and reports the results of Jesus' life and ministry, particularly in the Epistles.

The Old Testament uses various means to reveal Jesus, including promises, appearances, foreshadowing types, and titles.

First, the Old Testament teaches about Jesus in the numerous prophetic promises given about Him. More than one-quarter of the Old Testament was prophetic in nature,

---

[a] Luke 24:27 [b] Luke 24:44 [c] Luke 24:45 [d] E.g., Matt. 26:56; Luke 4:20–21; 22:37

promising future events. No other world religion or cult can present any specific prophecies concerning the coming of their prophets. However, in the Old Testament, we see hundreds of fulfilled prophecies extending hundreds and sometimes over a thousand years into the future, showing God's foreknowledge of and sovereignty over the future.

Second, the Old Testament teaches about Jesus through appearances that He makes before His birth, also called Christophanies. Examples include walking with Abraham, wrestling with Jacob, appearing to Moses, joining Shadrach, Meshach, and Abednego in the fiery furnace, and calling Isaiah into ministry.[a] Other examples may include "the angel [messenger] of the LORD," who is sometimes identified as God.[b] This angel provided the sacrifice in Isaac's place and spoke and journeyed with Moses.[c]

Third, types are Old Testament representative figures, institutions, or events that foreshadow Jesus. Examples include Adam, who foreshadows Jesus, the second Adam; the priesthood, prefiguring Jesus as our high priest; David and other kings, prefiguring Jesus as the King of Kings; Moses and the prophets, prefiguring Jesus as our ultimate prophet; animal sacrifices, prefiguring Jesus as the sinless Lamb of God slain for our sins; the temple, prefiguring God's presence dwelling among us in Jesus; shepherds reminding us sheep that Jesus is our Good Shepherd; judges, foreshadowing Jesus as the final judge of all people; and many others, such as Jesus, the true bread, true vine, and true light.

We also see people in the Old Testament who perform various kinds of service that is analogous to the service that Jesus performs perfectly. Unlike the first Adam, Jesus Christ is the Last Adam who passed His test in a garden and, in so doing, imputed His righteousness to us to overcome the sin imputed to us through the sin of the first Adam. Jesus is the true and better Abel who, although He was innocent, was slain and whose blood cries out. When Abraham left his father and home, he was doing the same thing that Jesus would do when He left Heaven. When Isaac carried

---

[a] Genesis 18, cf. John 8:56; Gen. 32:30; Ex. 3:2–6, cf. John 8:58; Dan. 3:24–25; Isa. 6:1–5; cf. John 12:41
[b] Judg. 6:11–21, 13:22 [c] Gen. 22:9–14; Ex. 3:14, 23:20–21, cf. John 8:56–59

the wood for his own sacrifice and was willing to lay down his life at the hand of his father Abraham, he was showing us what Jesus would later do. Jesus is the greater Jacob, wrestling with God in Gethsemane and, though wounded and limping, walked away from His grave blessed. Jesus is the greater Joseph, serving at the right hand of God the King, extending forgiveness and provision to those of us who have betrayed Him, and using His power to save us for loving reconciliation. Jesus is greater than Moses, standing as a mediator between God and us, bringing us the New Covenant.

Like Job, innocent Jesus suffered and was tormented by the Devil so that God might be glorified, while His foolish friends were no help or encouragement. Jesus is a King greater than David; He has slain our giants of Satan, sin, and death, although in the eyes of the world He was certain to face a crushing defeat at their hands. Jesus is greater than Jonah in that He spent three days in the grave, not just in a fish, to save a multitude even greater than Nineveh. When Boaz redeemed Ruth and brought her and her despised people into community with God's people, he was showing what Jesus would do to redeem His bride, the Church, from all the nations of the earth. When Nehemiah rebuilt Jerusalem, he was doing something like Jesus, who is building for us a New Jerusalem as our eternal home. When Hosea married an unfaithful wife that he continued to pursue in love, he was showing us the heart of Jesus, who does the same for His unfaithful bride, the Church.

We also see various Old Testament events preparing people for the coming of Jesus Christ. For example, in the Exodus account of Passover, the people placed blood over the doorframe of their home with hyssop (a common herb bundled for cleaning), and no one was to leave their home until the morning. Death would not come to any home marked with lamb's blood. 1 Peter 1:2 says our salvation is given by Jesus Christ and "...sprinkling with his blood..."

Fourth, there are many titles for God in the Old Testament that refer to Jesus Christ as God. In Daniel 7:13–14, God is called the "Son of Man," and Jesus adopted that as His favorite title, using it some 80 times in the four Gospels.

Jesus is the Suffering Servant that was promised in Isaiah.[a] Jesus is also known by many other Old Testament titles for God, including "first and...last," "light," "rock," "husband" or "bridegroom," "shepherd," "redeemer," "savior," "ransom," and "the Lord [of] glory."[b]

To properly understand the Old Testament, we must connect it to the person and work of Jesus. This should not be done in an allegorizing manner where arbitrary meanings foreign to Scripture are assigned to Old Testament words and images, thereby changing their meaning. Rather, the meaning of the Old Testament includes symbolism and identity that are most fully revealed in Jesus.

Unless Jesus is the central message of the Scriptures, errors abound. The most common is moralizing. Moralizing is reading the Bible not to learn about Jesus but only to learn principles for how to live life as a good person by following the good examples of some people and avoiding the bad examples of others. That kind of approach to the Scriptures is not Christian, because it treats the Bible like any other book with moral lessons that are utterly disconnected from faith in Jesus, salvation from Jesus, and life empowered by the same Holy Spirit of Jesus. All these themes connecting the Old Testament to the person and work of Jesus Christ culminate in the book of Hebrews, which we will learn more about studying next.

---

[a] Isa. 42:1–4, 49:1–7, 52:13–53:12, cf. Phil. 2:1–11 [b] Isa. 41:4, 44:6, 48:12; cf. Rev. 1:17, 2:8; Ps. 27:1, cf. John 1:9; Ps. 18:2, 95:1, cf. 1 Cor.10:4; 1 Pet. 2:6–8; Hos. 2:16; Isa. 62:5, cf. Eph. 5:28–33; Rev. 21:2.; Ps. 23:1, cf. Heb. 13:20; Hos. 13:14; Ps. 130:7, cf. Titus 2:13; Rev. 5:9; Isa. 43:3, cf. John 4:42; Isa. 42:8, cf. 1 Cor. 2:8

CHAPTER 3
10 TIPS FOR STUDYING HEBREWS

In most of the New Testament books, the human author and the intended first recipients of each book are clearly stated. However, that is not the case with Hebrews. There are numerous mysteries with Hebrews and several particular ways it's unique among books in the New Testament.

One, we don't know who the human author is that the Holy Spirit wrote through. The author makes no claim to be an Apostle (or eyewitness) to Jesus' earthly ministry. The only hint we have is that the author of Hebrews was a second-generation believer, as Hebrews 2:3 says, "It was declared at first by the Lord, and it was attested to us by those who heard..." The debate over who wrote Hebrews has been ongoing throughout church history. A Bible Dictionary says,

> Many early church fathers considered Paul the author. Tertullian (ca. ad 160–230) of Carthage in North Africa attributed Hebrews to Barnabas... Jerome noted that Gaius, bishop of Rome (d. ca. ad 217), denied Paul's authorship of Hebrews... Origen observed that the style of Hebrews was superior to that of Paul's. He also conceded that the thoughts were admirable and not inferior to Paul's acknowledged letters. He concluded, "I should say that the thoughts are those of the apostle, but the diction and phraseology are those of someone who remembered the apostolic teachings, and wrote down at his leisure what had been said by his teacher. Therefore if any church holds that this epistle is by Paul, let it be commended for this. For not without reason have the ancients handed it down as Paul's. But who wrote the epistle, in truth, God knows"... Origen further noted that tradition suggested either Clement of Rome or Luke, the author of Acts, as authors...The German Reformer Martin Luther (ad 1483–1546) suggested Apollos as its author... Twentieth-century scholars...[including] Paul Ellingworth considers this "the least unlikely of the

conjectures which have been put forward"... The prominent German scholar Adolf von Harnack (1851–1930), proposed Priscilla and Aquila as its co-authors... William Ramsay (1851–1939), a noted archaeologist of ancient Asia Minor, offered Philip the Evangelist as a possibility... Additional speculation includes Silvanus (Silas)..., Timothy..., Mary the Mother of Jesus..., and Pricilla...[5]

Two, we don't know exactly who the original audience was. Whoever penned Hebrews was known to its recipients.[a] The relationship between the author and recipients is warm enough that they are called brothers[b] and "beloved" or "dear" friends [c]. Furthermore, the author on one occasion in the letter refers to himself in the male gender.[d] Also, the author is close with Timothy, who was also part of Paul's ministry.[e] Therefore, it seems best to conclude that a well-known, respected, male early Church leader wrote the letter that was received as authoritative and ultimately from the Holy Spirit by the believers who first read it.

Three, we don't know exactly what kind of literature it is. In the New Testament, the epistles follow the classic ancient pattern of a letter with an introduction by the author, mention of the recipients, a body of the letter, and a customary conclusion. However, this format is not the case with Hebrews. As a Bible Dictionary says it,

> Lacks typical introduction with author and audience as is common in NT In both ancient and modern titles, Hebrews is commonly designated as a letter or an epistle. Origen (ca. ad 185–254), an early church father trained in classical rhetoric, characterized it as an "epistle"... In more recent years, it, "further notes that it has been classified as an epistle for most of its history..."[6]

Some Bible scholars have argued that Hebrews reads like the written manuscript of a magnificent sermon and that it may have been written with the intent of being read in its entirety as a sermon in various local churches. Perhaps it

[a] Hebrews 13:18-19, 22-23b [b] Hebrews 2:11, 10:19 [c] Hebrews 6:9 [d] Hebrews 11:32 [e] Hebrews 13:23

is best to regard Hebrews as a combination of sermon and letter, having originally been a sermon that was sent as a letter to be read from the pulpit in local churches.

Four, we don't know exactly when it was written. There are no clear historical details contained within Hebrews that help us narrow the window of possibility on when it was written.

Five, we do know that Hebrews is incredibly deep, rich, and profound. As one Bible dictionary says,

> Hebrews is a theologically rich document. Frank J. Matera considers the author of Hebrews "one of the great theologians of the New Testament, comparable to Paul and John in the depth of his theological insight"... Luke Timothy Johnson observes that "Hebrews is one of the most beautifully written, powerfully argued, and theologically profound writings in the New Testament..."[7]

Six, in Hebrews, we hear stark warnings

> that are supposed to bring us into a deeper fear of the Lord and obedience to God's commands...In the NT apostasy occurs when people turn aside from following Jesus (Jn. 6:66) and deny him after having previously confessed him as Lord. It manifests itself in falling away from faith under persecution (Matt. 24:9-13), denying the deity of Christ (1 Jn. 2:22), or living a life of open sin that denies the faith (2 Pet. 2:20). It is characteristic of the last days (2 Thess. 2:3; 1 Tim. 4:1; 2 Tim. 3:1, 5; 4:3-4...)."[8]

The timeliness of Hebrews is very much needed today because,

> The author of Hebrews issues a series of strong warnings about shrinking back or falling away, which he views as a most serious matter. The exact scope of the warning passages is a matter of some debate.... The author uses different terminology in his warnings... including "fall away" (ἀφίστημι, *aphistēmi*; Heb 3:12), "fall" (πίπτω, *piptō*;

Heb 3:17; 4:11), "fall away" or "commit apostasy" (παραπίπτω, *parapiptō*; Heb 6:6), "lose" or "throw away" (ἀποβάλλω, *apoballō*; Heb 10:35), and "refuse" (παραιτέομαι, *paraiteomai*; Heb 12:25).[9]

The people who originally received Hebrews had apparently stopped listening to God and godly Bible teaching, were not growing in their faith, and had reverted to questioning the foundational truths they had been taught as new Christians. Sadly, this very thing is happening today. By caving into cultural pressure, giving in to personal temptation for sexual sin, and trying to create a new kind of progressive Christianity, the same demonic spirit has seduced and sidetracked many people today as happened in the days of Hebrews. Hebrews 5:11-14 says,

> About this we have much to say, and it is hard to explain, since you have become dull of hearing. For though by this time you ought to be teachers, you need someone to teach you again the basic principles of the oracles of God. You need milk, not solid food, for everyone who lives on milk is unskilled in the word of righteousness, since he is a child. But solid food is for the mature, for those who have their powers of discernment trained by constant practice to distinguish good from evil.

Seven, Hebrews encourages us to think in terms of eternity. In life, everyone has some very rough days. Life has a way of knocking everyone down at some point and knocking most of us out at other points. The key in these toughest moments is to not be short-sighted, reacting out of fear or frustration. Instead, we need to take a deep breath, get some time with God to pray and listen, clear our mind, and keep eternity in sight. A friend of mine once said we should reverse engineer life. By that, he meant to start with the end in mind and then work backwards from our eternal goal to put our life together. If we know that Jesus is returning, we know we will rise from the dead, receive our eternal rewards, and live forever under King Jesus. If you are on Team Jesus, in the end, you are on the winning team and just need to persevere until all is said and done. Hebrews

continually points us towards eternity:
- 1:2 – ...in these last days he has spoken to us by his Son, whom he appointed the heir of all things, through whom also he created the world.
- 9:26b – ...he has appeared once for all at the end of the ages to put away sin by the sacrifice of himself.
- 10:37 – For, "Yet a little while, and the coming one will come and will not delay..."
- 10:38-39 – "...my righteous one shall live by faith, and if he shrinks back, my soul has no pleasure in him." But we are not of those who shrink back and are destroyed, but of those who have faith and preserve their souls.
- 11:16 – But as it is, they desire a better country, that is, a heavenly one. Therefore God is not ashamed to be called their God, for he has prepared for them a city.
- 13:14 – For here we have no lasting city, but we seek the city that is to come.

The big idea in living for eternity is to remind ourselves continually that what God has planned for us to enjoy with Him forever so far supersedes everything this life and world has to offer that there is simply no comparison. For this reason, a major theme of Hebrews is to patiently wait for what is "better," "greater," and "superior".[a]

Eight, the only way to rightly interpret the entire Bible, including the Old Testament, is to connect everyone and everything to the person and work of Jesus Christ. Hebrews refers to Jesus in numerous ways:
- Jesus Christ is referred to as the "Son"[b] and the "Son of God"[c]
- Jesus is the Word of God[d]
- Jesus is revealed in glory at the exalted right hand of God the Father[e]
- Jesus is referred to as sovereign "Lord"[f]
- Jesus' name appears repeatedly[g]
- Jesus is our leader and example of faith[h]
- Jesus as "priest" and "High Priest" appears dozens of

[a] Hebrews 1:4, 6:9, 7:7,19,22, 8:6, 9:23, 10:34, 11:16,35 [b] Hebrews 1:2, 5, 8; 7:28 [c] Hebrews 4:14; 6:6; 7:3; 10:29 [d] Hebrews 1:1-3 [e] Hebrews 1:3-4, 13; 8:1; 10:12-13; 12:2 [f] Hebrews 1:10; 2:3; 7:14; 13:20 [g] Hebrews 2:9; 3:1, 3; 5:7; 6:20; 7:22; 10:19; 12:2, 24; 13:12 [h] Hebrews 2:10; 4:14; 12:1-2

times[a]
- Jesus is revealed as Apostle one time[b]
- Combining His name and divine authority, we read of "Jesus, the Son of God"[c]
- Jesus is repeatedly revealed as the New Covenant sacrifice for sin across three chapters in the final half of the book[d]
- Jesus is the mediator between us and the Father in the New Covenant[e]
- "Jesus Christ" appears multiple times[f]

Nine, you cannot make sense of the New Testament, especially Hebrews, without understanding the Old Testament. Because the New Testament has roughly 300 explicit Old Testament quotations, as well as upwards of 4,000 Old Testament allusions, it is not surprising to find that the New Testament also has much to say about the Old Testament. These statements can be grouped into three general categories.

First, the New Testament clearly, repeatedly, and emphatically declares that the Old Testament is divinely inspired, sacred Scripture and the very words of God.[g]

Second, the New Testament makes many statements about the truthfulness and usefulness of the Old Testament. For example, the Old Testament comes with God's power[h], was written by God's inspiration[i], is sufficient for all that we truly need to know about God[j], is true and the source of truth[k], is for all people regardless of their culture or nation[l], is necessary to raise children[m], and ultimately is to be obeyed so that it is not merely a source of information but rather a means of transformation[n].

Third, like the Old Testament itself, the New Testament uses poetic images to reveal to us how we are to receive the Old Testament. The Old Testament is a sword for battle against Satan, sin, and demons[o], a seed that God plants in us that grows up as a life of fruitfully faithful living[p], and milk

---

[a] Hebrews 2:17; 3:1; 4:14-15; 5:1-6; 6:20; 7:1-28; 8:1-4; 9:11-14, 25; 10:11-18, 21 [b] Hebrews 3:1 [c] Hebrews 4:14 [d] Hebrews 8-10 [e] Hebrews 8:6, 8, 13; 9:11-15 [f] Hebrews 10:10; 13:8, 21 [g] Matt. 21:42, 22:29, 26:54,56; Luke 24:25-32, 44-45; John 5:39, 10:35; Acts 17:2,11, 18:28; Rom. 1:2, 4:3, 9:17, 10:11, 11:2, 15:4, 16:26; 1 Cor. 15:3-4; Gal. 3:8,22, 4:30; 1 Tim. 5:18; 2 Tim. 3:16; 2 Pet. 1:20-21, 3:15-16 [h] Heb. 4:12 [i] 2 Tim. 3:16; 2 Pet. 1:19-21 [j] Luke 16:29-31 [k] John 17:17 [l] Rom. 16:26 [m] 2 Tim. 3:15 [n] James 1:22 [o] Eph. 6:17; Heb. 4:12 [p] Luke 8:11-15

that nourishes us for life and growth, not unlike the feeding of a newborn baby [a]. Having studied what the Old and New Testaments say about the Old Testament, we will now examine what Jesus Himself said about it as our final point of study in this chapter.

Ten, Jesus taught us to trust the Old Testament. Jesus summarized the Old Testament Scripture as existing in three parts: the Law, Prophets, and Psalms.[b] He accepted the Old Testament canon as it exists today without any modifications and came to fulfill it.[c] As a rabbi (or preacher and teacher of Scripture), Jesus' entire ministry involved the instruction and application of the Old Testament. Jesus' public ministry even began with Him reading from the Old Testament book of Isaiah and stating that His ministry was to fulfill the Old Testament promises about His coming.[d]

Jesus clearly stated that His ministry was an Old Testament ministry in that it was to fulfill all of the Old Testament promises and longings that pointed to Him. Consequently, it is impossible to be a faithful Christian and not fully embrace the Old Testament as God's Word. Occasionally, someone will claim to be a Christian yet not embrace all of the Old Testament. One example is an ancient heretic (false teacher) named Marcion. He said that the Old Testament was in fact a far lesser book than the New Testament and encouraged Christians to remove it from their Bible. Unlike Marcion, however, Jesus clearly accepted and taught the Old Testament as sacred Scripture without reservation. Subsequently, we must either accept Rabbi Jesus as our most trustworthy Old Testament teacher or confess that he was a poor Bible teacher who made errors—and in turn elevate some other teacher over Him that we trust more fully. Jesus, the Rabbi/bible teacher, gives us multiple reasons to trust the Old Testament Scriptures He taught.

First, the parts of the Old Testament that are most commonly rejected as erroneous are also those sections of Scripture that Jesus clearly taught. This includes the literalness of Genesis 1-2[e], Cain and the murder of Abel[f], Noah and the flood[g], Abraham[h], Sodom and Gomorrah[i], Lot[j],

---

[a] 1 Pet. 2:2 [b] Luke 24:44 [c] Matt. 5:17 [d] Luke 4:16–21 [e] Matt. 19:4–5; Mark 10:6–8 [f] Matt. 23:35; Luke 11:51 [g] Matt. 24:37–39; Luke 17:26–27 [h] John 8:56 [i] Matt. 10:15, 11:23–24; Luke 10:12; 17:29 [j] Luke 17:28–32

Isaac and Jacob[a], the manna[b], the wilderness serpent[c], Moses as lawgiver[d], the popularity of the false prophets[e], and Jonah in the belly of a great fish[f].

Second, in matters of controversy, Jesus used the Old Testament as His court of appeals.[g] On many occasions, when an Old Testament teaching was questioned, Jesus simply believed the clear teaching of Old Testament Scripture and defended Himself by saying, "It is written."[h]

Third, in times of crisis, Jesus quoted from the Old Testament, indicating that it was His source of truth, solace, and defense. For example, when tempted by Satan, Jesus quoted from the book of Deuteronomy.[i] At the moment of His death, Jesus quoted Psalm 22:1 [cf. Matt. 27:46; Mark 15:34], saying, "My God, my God, why have you forsaken me?" And breathing His last in Luke 23:46, Jesus quoted Psalm 31:5, saying, "Into your hands I commit my spirit."

Fourth, Jesus repeatedly taught that Old Testament prophecy had been fulfilled.[j]

Fifth, Jesus named the authors of some Old Testament books. Some of the most common critiques launched at the Old Testament are in regard to authorship. For example, many Old Testament "scholars" boldly claim that Moses did not pen any of the first five books of the Old Testament, or that two or three authors penned Isaiah—none of whom was actually Isaiah. But Jesus taught that Scripture was authored by Moses[k], Isaiah[l], David[m], and Daniel[n].

In summary, Jesus taught that the Old Testament was perfectly inspired and totally truthful Scripture. Jesus devoted His ministry to teaching the Old Testament, defending the Old Testament, fulfilling the Old Testament, and using the Old Testament. Having established the authorship of the Old Testament and reflecting upon what the Old Testament, New Testament, and Jesus have to say about the Old Testament, we will now examine the opening chapters of the New Testament book of Hebrews, which serves as a commentary on much of the Old Testament.

[a] Matt. 8:11; Luke 13:28 [b] John 6:31, 49, 58 [c] John 3:14 [d] Matt. 8:4, 19:8; Mark 1:44, 7:10, 10:5, 12:26; Luke 5:14, 20:37; John 5:46, 7:19 [e] Luke 6:26 [f] Matt. 12:40 [g] Matt. 5:17–20, 22:29, 23:23; Mark 12:24 [h] Matt. 4:4,6,10, 11:10, 21:13, 26:24,31; Mark 1:2, 7:6, 9:12ff., 11:17, 14:21,27; Luke 2:23, 4:4,8,10,17, 7:27, 10:26, 19:46, 22:37; John 2:17, 6:31,45, 8:17, 10:34 [i] Matt. 4:1–11, cf. Deut. 8:3; Deut. 6:13,16 [j] Matt. 11:10, cf. Luke 7:27; Matt. 26:24,31, cf. Mark 14:27; Matt. 26:53–56, cf. Mark 14:49; Mark 9:12–13, 14:21; Luke 4:21, 18:31–33, 21:22, 22:37, 24:25–27, 24:44–47; John 5:39–47; John 13:18; cf. Ps. 41:9; John 15:25, cf. Ps. 35:19; John 17:12 [k] Mark 7:10 [l] Matt. 13:14; Mark 7:6 [m] Mark 12:36 [n] Matt. 24:15

CHAPTER 4
HEBREWS 1-3 PERSONAL AND GROUP STUDY GUIDE

1. How Can I Hear from God? (Hebrews 1:1-14)

Scripture for Memorization and Meditation:
Hebrews 1:1-3 – Long ago, at many times and in many ways, God spoke to our fathers by the prophets, but in these last days he has spoken to us by his Son, whom he appointed the heir of all things, through whom also he created the world. He is the radiance of the glory of God and the exact imprint of his nature, and he upholds the universe by the word of his power.

Commentary:
    Consider for a moment all the technological progress that has occurred simply to improve human communication. Just the simple device called a smartphone that most people carry around allows us to have phone calls, texts, and emails; make voice memos; take photos and videos; and post communication online, including on social media platforms. All the innovation necessary to permit this level of communication is nothing compared to the greatest possible communication gap —the one between our Holy God and us sinful people. That gap is infinite and could only be filled by God.

    How does God speak?

    This is one of the most important questions you can answer. If you answer this question wrong, it's likely you will build your entire life on lies only to eventually watch it crumble.

    Hebrews opens by saying that God spoke in the past by prophets. These were people of God, filled with the Spirit of God, who communicated the Word of God either by speaking or writing or both. Their words were divine revelation —perfect messages from God to us. Every prophet and prophecy in the Old Testament were like a series of signs on a highway —all pointing to the coming of Jesus Christ.

Immediately, the spotlight of Hebrews is turned on to Jesus Christ as the very Son of God. We are told that He shares all the same divine attributes as God the Father, is the Creator of all things, and is also the Sustainer, holding Creation together by His power. We are reminded that Jesus left His throne of glory to come into human history humbly and to live and die for us sinners as our Savior. To summarize this staggering introductory portrait of Jesus Christ:

1. Jesus Christ is heir of all things
2. Jesus Christ is the Creator of all things
3. Jesus Christ, the Son of God, is the perfect radiance of the glory of God the Father
4. Jesus Christ, the Son of God, shares all the divine attributes with God the Father
5. Jesus Christ sustains all creation
6. Jesus Christ is the only Savior for mankind
7. Jesus Christ is the intercessor between us and the Father

Jesus is then compared to, and shown to be superior in every way to, angels. The Bible has a great deal to say about spiritual beings, speaking of them as angels, watchers, holy ones, the host of Heaven, sons of God, divine assembly, the gods, morning stars, glorious ones, and the armies of Heaven.[a] A Bible dictionary says, "angels are mentioned almost three hundred times in Scripture, and are only noticeably absent from books such as Ruth, Nehemiah, Esther, the letters of John, and James."[10]

To ensure that we do not mistake Jesus for an angel, the author of Hebrews then goes to great lengths to explain how Jesus is not an angel. For starters, angels are created by God and Jesus is their Creator God. Furthermore, no angel is the very Son of God, appointed to co-rule and reign from the throne of glory in the unseen realm at the right hand of God the Father. Lastly, angels do not share the same divine attributes of the Father like Jesus Christ since they are not Creator, all-knowing, all-powerful, all-present, unchangeable, sovereign, or to be worshiped.

Practically speaking, this all means that Jesus Christ is

---

[a] Daniel 4:17; Psalm 89:5; Deuteronomy 4:19–20; 1 Kings 22:19; 1 Samuel 1:11; Job 1:6, 38:7; Deuteronomy 32:8–9; Psalm 82:1,6, 89:6; Ezekiel 28:2; Job 38:7; 2 Peter 2:10; Jude 8; Revelation 19:14

not an angel. Sadly, cults like the Jehovah's Witnesses teach this very lie. Furthermore, we are to trust Jesus more than angels, as some fallen angels that have become demons used lies to found cults like Mormonism (the demon Moroni masquerading as an angel) and false religions like Islam (a demon masquerading as Gabriel). Lastly, we should not worship or become overly enamored with angels, as is common in pagan spiritualities, including the New Age, along with esoteric spirituality. Sadly, in every generation, there are people who do not want to be under God's authority but still want to be spiritual. The thought of having a personal guardian angel, or being able to exercise spiritual authority by deploying angels to obey our requests, is a bit like having divine staff at our service. This, tragically, leaves people who are seeking spirits but not the Holy Spirit open to demonic counterfeits and dark ways of manipulating the spirit realm with such things as witchcraft, sorcery, divination, and magic. We don't need any of these things; all we need is Jesus! That is the constant drumbeat of Hebrews.

It's hard to imagine a more jaw-dropping, heart-pounding, awe-inspiring revelation of Jesus Christ as He is today, in full glory, being worshiped by the angels who surround His throne as the Center of creation and who are sent out from there on missions to serve Him in the earth. A Bible commentary says,

> To sit at the right hand of royalty was regarded as a great honor and proved that someone was worthy of great respect. Treating one's conquered enemies as a footstool is a metaphor taken from the ancient practice of a conquering king placing his foot on the neck of a defeated king as a symbolic gesture of triumph. Why is Jesus sitting, rather than standing, at God's right hand? The book of Hebrews proceeds to answer this question. He has done his priestly work of purification for sin and now waits until the final judgment (Ps. 110:1). Jesus used Psalm 110:1 with reference to himself in Mark 14:62. Even the Jews of the first century a.d. understood Psalm 110 to refer to the Messiah.[11]

While Hebrews often looks back to Jesus' years on earth in humility to live without sin, die for our sin, and rise for our salvation, the emphasis is on Jesus' current glory and future glorious dominion over all as King and Lord. Those who originally heard Hebrews were struggling and suffering. What emboldened and encouraged their faith was looking to Jesus, who is in glory today and is coming again in full authority as the object of our faith and the hope of our heart. The same is true for us. The more we can consistently keep Jesus Christ as the center of our focus and hope, seeing Him ruling and reigning right now in all glory with unlimited sovereign power, the more we are able to live by faith with joy as God intends.

Dig Deeper.
1. Read all of Hebrews in one sitting or over the course of a few days (this will take 45 minutes to an hour for most people).
2. Read Hebrews 1-3 at least once aloud to prepare to study this section of Scripture. Then, look up the Old Testament Scriptures that are quoted in this section of Hebrews (Psalm 2:7; 2 Samuel 7:14; Psalm 110:1; Deuteronomy 32:43; Psalm 45:6-7, 102:25-27, 110:1; 102:25-27).

Walk it out. Talk it out.
1. If the group is new or has any new group members, start by briefly having everyone introduce themselves.
2. What level of familiarity does everyone in the group have with Hebrews (e.g., are some people just reading it for the first time, have others read it in its' entirety, or have some even studied it)?
3. What are you hoping to learn, and how are you hoping to grow as you read and study Hebrews?
4. How can the group members be praying for each other?

NOTES

SHALLOW CHRISTIANITY?

2. Why is God Angry with Shallow Christians? (Hebrews 2:1-9)

Scripture for Memorization and Meditation:
Hebrews 2:1 – ...we must pay much closer attention to what we have heard, lest we drift away from it.

Commentary:

When our kids were little, we enjoyed spending our vacations on a lake a few hours from our house. After a fun day of riding a jet ski, we tied it up to the dock outside the home we were borrowing, ate dinner, and went to bed. When we turned on our phones the next morning, there was a voicemail from someone who found the jet ski on the shore of the complete opposite end of the lake. Apparently, the jet ski somehow became disconnected from the dock. It was surprising how quickly it drifted as far away as it possibly could.

Christians who stop reading their Bible, praying, repenting of sin, and gathering with fellow believers in a church are a lot like that jet ski. Quickly after becoming disconnected from these holy habits, we can drift far off course. This is precisely what this section of Hebrews warns against, urging us not to "drift away." Speaking of the original Greek text from which our English Bible translations are adapted, a Bible commentary says, "Our failure carefully to attend to what God is saying to us in the gospel of Christ is arrestingly explained with the use of a word (pararuōmen) which is used in other contexts to describe a boat which is allowed to drift away aimlessly, so missing the landing point."[12]

Technically, to "drift away" is referred to by Christian scholars as apostasy. A Bible Encyclopedia says, "Turning against God, as evidenced by abandonment and repudiation of former beliefs. The term generally refers to a deliberate renouncing of the faith by a once sincere believer rather than a state of ignorance or mistaken knowledge."[13]

Today, apostasy is rampant —from deconstructionists who are former Christians devoted to dismantling the faith to mainline Protestant denominations supporting same-sex marriage and transgenderism, Bible colleges and seminaries that deny the necessity of Jesus Christ for salvation and the literalness of eternal Hell, any church that flies a rainbow flag, and any Christian that promotes tolerance of sin instead of repentance of sin. Younger generations in particular, fearing a backlash from an increasingly hostile secular culture, are prone to apostasy by abandoning clear Bible teaching.

Hebrews is filled with warnings against apostasy, with the section of Scripture we are studying serving as the first of five warnings.

- Warning 1: Do not abandon God's Word[a]
- Warning 2: Do not become hard-hearted and start ignoring God[b]
- Warning 3: Do not settle for being spiritually immature and stop growing[c]
- Warning 4: Do not become disloyal and turn your back on Jesus Christ[d]
- Warning 5: Do not reject God's Word and His authority over your life[e]

For those who have spent time in the church, perhaps growing up in a Christian home, the things of God can become too familiar. If there is not sufficient teaching about the holiness of God, the horror of sin, and rightful fear of the Lord, Jesus can be turned into little more than a buddy or motivational life coach —no one you should revere, fear, or obey. When our view of Jesus is low, our view of ourselves becomes high. We start to think we are better and smarter than God says we are. In this section of Scripture, we are reminded of the greatness of God, which should cause in us a holy fear and reverence of the Lord.

We are reminded of both Jesus' words and works. In word, Jesus preached to the world that He alone is God and He had come down from Heaven to live without sin, die for our sin, and rise as the "Founder of Salvation." In work, Jesus proved His claims, "by signs and wonders and various miracles." Furthermore, the confirmation of Jesus as God and Lord was made by both the Father, as, "God also bore witness," and "the Holy Spirit," who did powerful miracles

[a] Hebrews 2:1–4 [b] Hebrews 3:7-4:13 [c] Hebrews 5:11-6:12 [d] Hebrews 10:19-39 [e] Hebrews 12:14-29

with Jesus to verify His majesty and authority.

The author of Hebrews then asks a very sobering, humbling, and clarifying question, "What is man, that you are mindful of him, or the son of man, that you care for him?" For a moment, consider the history of the human race from God's perspective. He created us, blessed us, and gave us one command, and we sinned against Him, which cursed everyone and everything. God owes us nothing, and the truth is we are simply not a big deal. When angels sinned, as we did, they became demons, and God did nothing to seek and save them. Human beings are "lower than the angels," yet God came as one of us to suffer and die as our Savior. Furthermore, we are told that God has a long history of punishing rebels, which should make us take seriously any sinful drifting in our own lives.

Sadly, the drift away from deeply anchored Christianity is largely caused by weak pulpits. In boating, a buoy is supposed to be anchored to the bottom of a lake or ocean so that boats can tie on to that buoy, which keeps them from drifting away. In the church, the pulpit is supposed to be like that buoy. The preacher and the preaching are supposed to be immovable and unwavering so that the people in the church can tie the boats holding their families to a firm buoy. Tragically, when the preacher and preaching are not anchored and begin to drift, the entire church begins to scatter and drift away. Additionally, rebellious people who do have a strong, dependable pulpit sometimes intentionally unhook their boat so they can drift away into sin and folly. Either way, once this drift begins, a crisis is set in motion as Hebrews soberly warns against.

Dig Deeper.
1. Look up and read the 5 warnings in Hebrews for yourself (2:1-4, 3:7-4:13, 5:11-6:12, 10:19-39, 12:14-29).
2. Pray and humbly ask the Holy Spirit if any of these warnings are specifically speaking to you about an area in your life where you are drifting away.

Walk it out. Talk it out.
Ask people in the group to share any testimony of a time in their own life when they drifted away and how they came

back to a fear of God and genuine faith.

NOTES

3. How Do I Overcome Suffering and Temptation? (Hebrews 2:10-18)

Scripture for Memorization and Meditation:
Hebrews 2:17-18 – Therefore he had to be made like his brothers in every respect, so that he might become a merciful and faithful high priest in the service of God, to make propitiation for the sins of the people. For because he himself has suffered when tempted, he is able to help those who are being tempted.

Commentary:
Suffering.

Christians often deal with suffering by looking forward to the eternal state after Jesus returns, the dead are raised, the curse is lifted, and suffering is forever gone because sin is no more. We who are suffering long for the day when the suffering will end once and for all.

On the flip side, God has never sinned and, as a result, has caused Himself no suffering. However, God chose to leave His perfect, sinless reality to enter into our sinful history and suffer for our sins.

Perhaps you have heard so much about Jesus Christ as God becoming a man to suffer and die for you that it has somehow lost its astonishment. Consider, for a moment, that you had a wonderful life but chose to give it all up to go and let your enemies torment and harm you, eventually murdering you, even though they don't ask for it or, in any way, deserve it. As sinners, we were God's enemies, and He chose to freely and lovingly come into our sinful world and suffer at the hands of sinful men and women, ultimately dying to rescue us from the wrath of God we fully deserve.

Perhaps you might suffer and die for someone you love and who loves you. However, can you even imagine suffering and dying for someone who hates you? That's what Jesus Christ did on His rescue mission to our rebellious planet.

In the context of Hebrews 2, the author is teaching about the unique gift that human beings receive that divine beings do not. According to the storyline of the Bible, God is the Creator of both human and divine beings (also called angels). Both human and divine beings sinned and rebelled against God. Jesus Christ came as a human being in "flesh and blood" to provide "salvation" through His "death" and deliver us from "sin," "death," and "the devil." Jesus accomplished all of this, we are told, through His "propitiation for the sins of the people."

In this section of Hebrews, we are introduced to Jesus' work as "priest" and "High Priest," which are major themes throughout the book. Hebrews 2:17-18 says, "Therefore he had to be made like his brothers in every respect, so that he might become a merciful and faithful high priest in the service of God, to make propitiation for the sins of the people. For because he himself has suffered when tempted, he is able to help those who are being tempted."

A Bible dictionary says,

> In the Old Testament, the primary purpose of the high priest was to serve as a representative and mediator between the people and Yahweh. The office was established with Aaron, the brother of Moses, and high priests were the head priest first at the tabernacle and then later at the temple...The high priest served several purposes that were crucial to Israelite worship. It was the high priest's responsibility to see that the covenant was enforced, and to direct people to complete the duties of the temple and the law of Moses. As the representative for the nation of Israel, the high priest had a tremendous responsibility to direct the hearts of the people toward God and the fulfillment of the covenant. Some of the primary responsibilities of the high priest were the regular handling of sacrifices and offerings, the blessing of people, and the annual entrance into the most holy place within the tabernacle/temple during the Day of Atonement.[14]

Among the central events in the Old Testament was the act of atonement, including the annual celebration of the Day of Atonement (Yom Kippur) according to the regulations of the book of Leviticus.

The Day of Atonement was the most important day of the year. It was intended to deal with the sin problem between humanity and God. Of the many prophetic elements on this special day, one stands out. On that day, two healthy goats without defect were chosen; they were therefore fit to represent sinless perfection, perhaps in spite of the protests of animal rights activists.

The first goat was a sin offering. The high priest slaughtered this innocent goat, which acted as a substitute for the sinners who rightly deserved a violently bloody death for their many sins. He then sprinkled some of its blood on the mercy seat on top of the Ark of the Covenant inside the Holy of Holies. The goat was no longer innocent when it took the guilt of sin; it was a sin offering for the people.[a] Subsequently, its blood represented life given as payment for sin. The dwelling place of God was thus cleansed of the defilement that resulted from all the transgressions and sins of the people of Israel, and God's just and holy wrath was satisfied. Theologically, we call this the doctrine of *propitiation*, whereby God's wrath is propitiated (or taken from us) because of Jesus so that we are no longer under God's wrath.

Then the high priest, acting as the representative and mediator between the sinful people and their holy God, would take the second goat and lay his hands on the animal while confessing the sins of the people. This goat, called the scapegoat, would then be sent away to run free into the wilderness away from the sinners, symbolically taking their sins with it. Theologically, we call this the doctrine of *expiation*, whereby our sin is expiated (or taken away) so that we are made clean.

In summary, all of this foreshadowed the coming of Jesus Christ, our High Priest, who mediates between unholy people and our holy God, the sinless substitute who died a bloody death in our place for our sins, and the scapegoat who takes our sins away to be remembered by God no more. Subsequently, only by rightly understanding the function of the two goats is the atonement fully appreciated. Although there were two goats, there was only one slaughter. The first goat was slaughtered for the propitiation of sin. The second goat was not slaughtered but rather sent away with sin, showing the cleansing expiation from sin. Both great themes, propitiation and expiation, will be further explored

---

[a] Lev. 6:15

in separate chapters in this book.

These great images of the priest, slaughter, and scapegoat are all given by God to help us more fully comprehend Jesus' work for us on the cross. Theologically, this is called *atonement* (or at-one-ment); Jesus, our God, became a man to restore a relationship between God and humanity. This is also what is meant throughout the English Standard Version of the Bible when the word *atone* and its related variations (such as *atoned* and *atonement*) appear nearly 100 times.

Jesus Christ is God who understands us, has suffered like us, and has been tempted like us. He fully, completely, and totally knows how every day in this fallen, cursed, demonic world is a battle for a believer to walk with God. When you are tempted to sin and suffering in any way, you can speak with Jesus Christ, who hears and answers you and fully understands what you are experiencing, because He has been through what you are going through, gotten to the other side, and will walk with you through it into victory! Admittedly, this section causes some people confusion because it clearly says Jesus was tempted, yet James 1:13 says that "...God cannot be tempted with evil..." When Jesus humbled Himself and became a man, He did not lose any of His divine attributes. However, He temporarily chose not to use them. In the same way, a shooter can also wear a blindfold for a shot, and they do not lose their sight but rather simply choose not to use it. God is all-present, but for a season, Jesus chose to live in a body and travel from one place to another. God does not change, but for a season, Jesus chose to go through the same physical process that we all do from baby in the womb to adult. And, God is not tempted, but for the season in which He was living on earth like us, Jesus chose to endure temptation like we do. You can read of this for yourself in Luke 4:1-13, where Satan himself showed up to tempt Jesus.

In suffering and temptation, we are also told that Jesus was made "perfect through suffering." This does not mean that somehow Jesus was sinfully imperfect. Instead, the author of Hebrews is referring to two kinds of learning. One, we learn by instruction and observation. Two, we learn through experience. In the former, we can, for example, learn about marriage or parenting or suffering by reading books and talking with people who have life experience in those areas. In the latter, we go through those experiences for ourselves to find that being married, raising a child, or battling cancer is very different than reading about it in a book. Jesus knew about suffering and temptation, watched humanity endure both, but then had a deeper level of learning when He experienced both for Himself. He now knows about what each of us is going through to a depth that is so helpful that no one can compare to the depth of help Jesus is for every season of this life.

Lastly, we are told that God's goal for each of His children is to get us "to glory." Being saved, baptized, and starting our Christian walk is the finish line, not the starting line. Too many Christians make salvation their finish line, as if repenting of sin and receiving Jesus was the end of our walk with God. God's goal is, and our goal must be, to keep growing in glory by learning, suffering, repenting, and maturing until the perfect version of us is unveiled in the Kingdom. There, like a mirror reflects an image, we will reflect the goodness and glory of Christ forever and ever in our character. The exhortation is to not stop maturing and not settle for anything less than getting "to glory."

Dig Deeper.
1. Look up the following Old Testament Scriptures that are quoted in this section of Hebrews: Psalm 8:4-6, 8:17-18, 22:22; Isaiah 8:17-8.
2. Since the theme of Jesus as priest is introduced here and central to the book of Hebrews, look up the other times this occurs in the book (2:17, 3:1, 4:14-15, 5:1-10, 6:20, 7:1-28, 8:1-4, 9:6-11, 9:25, 10:11, 10:21, 13:11).

Walk it out. Talk it out.
1. What did the Holy Spirit highlight in this section of Hebrews for you? Why?
2. What did you learn, or learn more about, regarding the ministry of Jesus Christ in this section of Hebrews?
3. How does understanding Jesus as a faithful and merciful High Priest who fully understands and sympathizes with your suffering and temptation help

you pray and worship Him better?
4. How can group members be praying for each other this week?

NOTES

4. How is Jesus the Hero of the Whole Bible? (Hebrews 3:1-6)

Scripture for Memorization and Meditation:
Hebrews 3:6 – ...but Christ is faithful over God's house as a son. And we are his house, if indeed we hold fast our confidence and our boasting in our hope.

Commentary:
　　In the Bible, there are people who loom so large that it's hard to overstate the impact of their life. Moses is one of those men. He is referred to or alluded to roughly 800 times in the Bible.
　　Moses' life began with his life being spared. Later, God speaks to Him through a burning bush, calling him into ministry. God works through Moses to take down the Egyptian empire with 10 plagues. God then uses Moses to liberate His people and parts the Red Sea to deliver them. Moses receives the 10 Commandments from God Himself. Moses then destroys the golden calf to defend God's honor. God uses Moses to help build the tabernacle to house His presence. Lastly, Moses pens the first five books of the Bible, giving us "the law," while leading God's people to the edge of the Promised Land. Moses' life is so epic that numerous major motion pictures have been made, along with many televised biographical series examining his life, as even non-religious people find him fascinating. Furthermore, "Moses (c. 1400 BCE) is considered one of the most important religious leaders in world history. He is claimed by the religions of Judaism, Christianity, Islam and Bahai as an important prophet of God and the founder of monotheistic belief."[15]
　　A Bible Dictionary describes Moses as,

> The man chosen by God to lead the Hebrew people out of Egyptian bondage, to preside over the Sinai ceremony constituting those people as the people of God, and to lead the Hebrew people to the promised land. As such, Moses is arguably the most prominent person in the Hebrew Bible, and he looms large in early Jewish and Christian writings.[16]

The relationship between Moses and Jesus Christ is evidenced in several places and ways throughout the Scriptures. In Deuteronomy 18:18, God said to Moses, "I will raise up for them a prophet like you from among their brothers. And I will put my words in his mouth, and he shall speak to them all that I command him." Over a millennium later, in Acts 3:17-22, Peter quoted Deuteronomy 18:18 and applied its fulfillment to Jesus Christ. Therefore, the relationship in this instance includes that Jesus' eventual coming was promised to Moses, that Jesus and Moses both occupied the office of prophet, that both Jesus and Moses were Hebrews, and that both Jesus and Moses spoke the words given to them by the Father.

In this section of Hebrews, we learn that Jesus and Moses were faithful to the Father's leading, but that Jesus is worthy of greater honor because He is much greater than even Moses. While Moses was faithful to help build God's house, Jesus is the "son" of God who owns God's house. Without diminishing or denigrating Moses, this section of Scripture elevates Jesus Christ to an infinitely greater and superior position of glory and authority.

And, in one of the more mysterious verses, we find that Jesus Christ was the motive and inspiration for Moses. Hebrews 11:26 (NIV) says, "He (Moses) regarded disgrace for the sake of Christ as of greater value than the treasures of Egypt, because he was looking ahead to his reward."

In this packed section of Scripture, we are reminded of four offices Jesus Christ holds that benefit us as believers.

One, Jesus is our "apostle." In the ancient world, an apostle or messenger was sent out from a King with full authority to speak and lead on his behalf. When sent to the earth by God the Father, Jesus Christ served as the perfect messenger and representative of the Kingdom of God. Practically, this means that He has unmatched authority.

Two, Jesus is our "high priest." As we have previously established in this study guide, this reveals Jesus as the compassionate connector between us and God the Father.

Three, Jesus is the "son" of God. Because Jesus is eternal and without an earthly father, the concept of Him as the Divine Son has nothing to do with a biological connection as is common with human fathers and sons. In the ancient world, the concept of a King with a son meant that the authority, dominion, power, and possessions belonged to the household with the son as rightful owner and heir. A Bible Dictionary says,

> In Hebrews, Jesus is "the Son," who is God's "firstborn" and personal "heir," who is creator and sustainer of the universe, and who is the "radiance of God's glory" (Heb 1:2–12; 3:6; 5:5). As the Son, he is the final and eternal High Priest who ascended to heaven and whose mediatorial work remains perfect forever (4:14; 6:6; 7:3, 28).[17]

The similarities between Moses and Jesus are many:
1. When Moses was a baby boy, the Egyptian government ordered the mass killing of Hebrew boys aged two and under. When Jesus was a boy, the Roman government did the exact same thing.
2. Moses grew up in Egypt as a boy. Jesus' family fled to Egypt, where He also grew up as a boy.
3. Moses was laid in a straw-thatched basket as a baby, and Jesus was laid in a straw-thatched manger as a baby.
4. Moses left his position of royalty to humbly serve people, and Jesus did the same when He came from Heaven to earth.
5. God spoke to Moses through a burning bush, and Jesus was the God who spoke.
6. God did supernatural signs and wonders to verify the ministry and authority of both Moses and Jesus.
7. Moses turned water into blood, and Jesus turned water into wine.
8. God parted the Red Sea for Moses, and God, as Jesus, calmed the Sea of Galilee.
9. Moses brought a nation out of demonic bondage into freedom so they could worship God, and Jesus has done the same for every nation.
10. Moses gave us the Law, and Jesus came to fulfill the Law.
11. Moses and Jesus both spent time in the wilderness to prepare for their respective ministries.

12. Moses chose 12 spies to serve his ministry, and Jesus chose 12 disciples to serve His ministry.
13. God supernaturally fed people in the days of Moses, and He did the same kind of thing, performing provision miracles of food in the days of Jesus.
14. Moses carried God's presence in the Ark of the Covenant, and Jesus carried God's presence in His body.
15. Jesus came down from Heaven to meet with Moses when he was on the earth, and Moses later came down from Heaven to meet with Jesus when He was on the earth.

Lastly, because of Jesus Christ, we are told that we are "holy brothers" with "a heavenly calling." Practically, this means that because of Jesus, believers in Him have their sins forgiven and erased, replaced with His perfect holiness gifted to us. Today, our life is the beginning of our heavenly calling, by living under the Lordship of Christ over every aspect of our life throughout life and into eternity.

Dig Deeper.
This week, read through the entire book of Hebrews and make note of the times it refers to Moses, events surrounding his life, or people and things he wrote about in Genesis, Exodus, Leviticus, Numbers, and Deuteronomy.

Walk it out. Talk it out.
1. When the Bible says you are "holy," how does that change how you view yourself as a Christian?
2. How are you growing to better understand Jesus as your High Priest who is right now interceding for you in prayer and cares for you?
3. Moses was a great leader of God's people. Who have you known that was a great leader of God's people?
4. How can the group be praying for one another this week?

NOTES

5. Does God Punish Some Believers? (Hebrews 3:7-19)

Scripture for Memorization and Meditation:
Hebrews 3:7-9 – Therefore, as the Holy Spirit says, "Today, if you hear his voice, do not harden your hearts as in the rebellion, on the day of testing in the wilderness, where your fathers put me to the test and saw my works for forty years."

Commentary:

Imagine that you live downstream from a toxic industrial plant that continually pollutes the water that runs through your property. What if you decided it was time to begin a cleanup effort? Where would you begin? Obviously, starting on your property, seeking to continually clean the water, would be a foolish waste of time. The only hope to cause real change would be to start upstream at the headwaters of the problem.

Our life is a lot like this story. Our behavior is downstream. Our heart is upstream. When the Bible speaks of our heart roughly 900 times, it is referring to the upstream emotional center from which floods our feelings, values, beliefs, decisions, and behaviors. Simply stated, the heart is upstream, and the rest of life is downstream. Proverbs 4:23 says, "Keep your heart with all vigilance, for from it flow the springs of life."

In this section of Hebrews, the focus is on our hearts. We are told, "Therefore, as the Holy Spirit says, 'Today, if you hear his voice, do not harden your hearts…'" The good news, we are told, is that the Holy Spirit speaks to us. He does this through such things as Scripture, our conscience, and godly wise counsel. The bad news is that we can, and sadly do, harden our own hearts.

The first reference to hardness of heart is written by Moses (featured in the prior section of Hebrews we just studied) in the book of Exodus in relation to the Pharaoh. Paul also speaks of this in Romans 9:14-18. The Israelite people, numbering a few million, were enslaved to a cruel tyrant named Pharaoh, who ruled as the most powerful man on earth and was worshiped as a god. God called Moses to proclaim to Pharaoh God's demand that His people be released to worship Him freely. The concept of the hardening of Pharaoh's heart is introduced by God in Exodus 4:21, "And the Lord said to Moses, 'When you go back to Egypt, see that you do before Pharaoh all the miracles that I have put in your power. But I will harden his heart, so that he will not let the people go.'" This theme of Pharaoh's hardness of heart is a subject that appears 19 more times in the rest of Exodus.[a] Some of these verses say that it was God who hardened Pharaoh's heart, while others indicate that Pharaoh hardened his own heart.

The question of how God hardened Pharaoh's heart is incredibly important if the justice of God is to be defended. The answer is that God hardened Pharaoh's heart with patience and grace. God did not need to send Moses to Pharaoh on multiple occasions to invite Pharaoh to repent of his sin and free the Israelites. God did not need to perform miracles in front of Pharaoh to prove His power and sovereign rule over even Pharaoh. Furthermore, God knew that Pharaoh's heart was hardened and that, in asking him to repent and come under the leadership of the real God, Pharaoh would only grow angrier and more hardhearted. Therefore, it was grace that hardened Pharaoh's heart, like heaping burning coals on the head of one's enemies, as Jesus said.

Subsequently, God remains gracious and is not unjust. The responsibility for the hard heart is ultimately the unrepentant, sinful Pharaoh, who repeatedly rejected God's offer of grace. Thus, the truism of the Puritans rings true that "the same sun that melts the ice hardens the clay." The author of Hebrews, along with Paul in Romans 9, is warning us that we are each like Pharaoh when we harden our own heart.

After Pharaoh's heart was hardened against God, he was dealt a severe judgment that included the taking of the life of his firstborn son and the destruction of his entire Kingdom by God. Seeing the wrath of God poured out because of hardness of heart, you would think that God's people, who were then set free to begin their journey home to the Promised Land, would diligently and personally guard against hardness of heart. Sadly, the author of Hebrews

---

[a] Exodus 7:3, 13, 14, 22; 8:15, 19, 32; 9:7, 12, 34–35; 10:1, 20, 27; 11:10; 13:15; 14:4, 8, 17

reminds us of the tragic tale in Exodus where God's people chose to "harden" their "hearts" in the wilderness where God says, "they put me to the test," "provoked" His anger, choosing to "go astray in their heart," because they had an "evil, unbelieving heart,, causing them to "fall away from the living God," becoming "hardened by the deceitfulness of sin," leading to living "disobedient" and in "unbelief." Despite God doing His miraculous "works for forty years," which included a cloud to lead them by day, a fire to lead them by night, and provision of food to sustain them, the people did not repent of their hardness of heart. As punishment, God let an entire generation die in the wilderness, never making it home to the Promised Land, which today is the nation of Israel.

The trip should have taken roughly 11 days. Deuteronomy 1:1-2 says, "These are the words that Moses spoke to all Israel beyond the Jordan in the wilderness...It is eleven days' journey from Horeb by the way of Mount Seir to Kadesh-barnea." Why did a journey that should have taken 11 days last 40 years? Because of hardness of heart.

When our heart is hard, we are not teachable and refuse to listen to God or any other wisdom for that matter. When our heart is hard, we become proud, and rather than following and obeying, we strike off on our own path into folly and harm. When our heart is hard, we do not acknowledge our wrongdoing, repent, and turn around, but rather keep going in the same wrong direction only to pay painful consequences. When our heart is hard, eventually it becomes nearly dead —incapable of feeling much of anything.

The story of the Exodus is part of the overarching gospel story of the Bible. Jesus is the greater Moses, who liberates us from Satan, who is the greater Pharaoh. We are delivered from a counterfeit kingdom of darkness and the demonic to Christ's Kingdom of light and life. Just as Moses led the people to freedom, Jesus has led us to freedom. Just as the people had to choose whether they would worship God on the journey to their home country headquartered by Jerusalem or harden their hearts in sin, we too are literally on our journey home to the Kingdom of God headquartered by the New Jerusalem and are responsible for the condition of our heart before God.

Is your heart hard in any way toward God or the things of God? Are there parts of the Bible you refuse to agree with, or any sin in your life that you refuse to put to death out of obedience to your God? Have you, in any way, used the excuse that because your life has been hard, you have a right for your heart to be hard? Are you blaming God for your hard heart rather than repenting of your hard heart and bringing it to God to get a new heart instead?

Dig Deeper.
Get some time alone with God and ask the Holy Spirit to reveal to you anything you need to repent of and see changed in your heart as you prayerfully and carefully read Psalms 51 and 139. Use a pad and pen to journal out whatever God brings to mind, and spend time speaking with Him honestly about your heart.

Walk it out. Talk it out.
1. Is anyone in the group willing to share a time that they had a hard heart and what that was like?
2. If each person in the group had to pick one word to describe their heart today, what word would they choose and why? (e.g., joyful, fearful, broken, healed, thankful, hard, confused, hopeful, etc.)
3. Looking back on the hardening of Pharaoh's heart in Exodus and Romans 9:14-18, what personal lessons can you learn about the hardening of his own heart in response to God's repeated correction of and consequence for sin?
4. How can group members be praying for one another this week?

NOTES

ENDNOTES

1. Warren W. Wiersbe, *Wiersbe's Expository Outlines on the New Testament* (Wheaton, IL: Victor Books, 1992), 674.
2. Derek R. Brown and E. Tod Twist, *Romans*, ed. Douglas Mangum, Lexham Research Commentaries (Bellingham, WA: Lexham Press, 2014), Ro 2:1–16.
3. Douglas R. De Lacey, "Gentiles," ed. Gerald F. Hawthorne, Ralph P. Martin, and Daniel G. Reid, *Dictionary of Paul and His Letters* (Downers Grove, IL: InterVarsity Press, 1993), 335.
4. James P. Sweeney, "Hebrews, Letter to the," ed. John D. Barry et al., *The Lexham Bible Dictionary* (Bellingham, WA: Lexham Press, 2016).
5. Ibid.
6. Ibid.
7. Ibid.
8. Moisés Silva and Merrill Chapin Tenney, *The Zondervan Encyclopedia of the Bible*, A-C (Grand Rapids, MI: The Zondervan Corporation, 2009), 253.
9. James P. Sweeney, "Hebrews, Letter to the," ed. John D. Barry et al., *The Lexham Bible Dictionary* (Bellingham, WA: Lexham Press, 2016).
10. R. K. Harrison, *Evangelical Dictionary of Biblical Theology*, Baker Reference Library, ed. Walter A. Elwell (Grand Rapids, MI: Baker Book House, 1996), 21.
11. Robert B. Hughes and J. Carl Laney, *Tyndale Concise Bible Commentary*, The Tyndale Reference Library (Wheaton, IL: Tyndale House Publishers, 2001), 664.
12. Raymond Brown, The Message of Hebrews: Christ above All, The Bible Speaks Today (Leicester, England; Downers Grove, IL: InterVarsity Press, 1988), 47.
13. James D. Price and Luder G. Whitlock Jr., "Apostasy," Baker Encyclopedia of the Bible

(Grand Rapids, MI: Baker Book House, 1988), 130.
14. Mary B. MacFarlane, "High Priest," ed. John D. Barry et al., *The Lexham Bible Dictionary* (Bellingham, WA: Lexham Press, 2016).
15. https://www.worldhistory.org/Moses/
16. David Noel Freedman, ed., "Moses (Person)," The Anchor Yale Bible Dictionary (New York: Doubleday, 1992), 909.
17. Walter A. Elwell and Philip Wesley Comfort, Tyndale Bible Dictionary, Tyndale Reference Library (Wheaton, IL: Tyndale House Publishers, 2001), 1214.

ABOUT MARK DRISCOLL AND REALFAITH

With Pastor Mark, it's all about Jesus! He is a spiritual leader, prolific author, and compelling speaker, but at his core, he is a family man. Mark and his wife Grace have been married and doing vocational ministry together since 1993 and, along with their five kids, planted Trinity Church in Scottsdale, Arizona as a family ministry. Among their five kids, three are married, and they have three grandsons and a granddaughter.

Pastor Mark, Grace, and their oldest daughter, Ashley, also started RealFaith Ministries, which contains a mountain of Bible teaching for men, women, couples, parents, pastors, leaders, Spanish speakers, and more, which you can access by visiting **RealFaith.com** or downloading the **RealFaith app**.

With a master's degree in exegetical theology from Western Seminary in Portland, Oregon, he has spent the better part of his life teaching verse-by-verse through books of the Bible, contextualizing its timeless truths and never shying away from challenging, convicting passages that speak to the heart of current cultural dilemmas.

Together, Mark and Grace have co-authored *Win Your War*, *Real Marriage*, and *Real Romance: Sex in the Song of Songs* and he co-authored a father-daughter project called *Pray Like Jesus* with his daughter, Ashley. Pastor Mark has also written numerous other books including *Vote Like Jesus*, *Act Like a Man*, *Spirit-Filled Jesus*, *Who Do You Think You Are?*, *Vintage Jesus*, and *Doctrine*.

If you have any prayer requests for us, questions for future Ask Pastor Mark or Dear Grace videos, or a testimony regarding how God has used this and other resources to help you learn God's Word, we would love to hear from you at **hello@realfaith.com**.

DOWNLOAD THE REALFAITH APP TO GET MORE BIBLE TEACHING FROM PASTOR MARK & GRACE.

WANT TO BUILD MOMENTUM IN YOUR PRAYER LIFE? LEARN TO "PRAY LIKE JESUS" WITH A FREE E-BOOK FROM PASTOR MARK & HIS OLDEST DAUGHTER, ASHLEY CHASE.

IT'S ALL ABOUT JESUS!

REALFAITH.COM